J'ACCUSE

J'ACCUSE

Aharon Shabtai

Translated by Peter Cole

 A NEW DIRECTIONS BOOK

Some of these poems were first published in the *London Review of Books, Parnassus in Review,* and *Modern Poetry in Translation.*

Manufactured in the United States of America
New Directions Books are printed on acid-free paper.
First published as New Directions Paperbook NDP in 2003
Published simultaneously in Canada by Penguin Books Canada Limited

LIBRARY OF CONGRESS CATALOGING IN PUBLICATION DATA
Shabtai, Aharon.
[Poems. English. Selections]
J'accuse / Aharon Shabtai ; translated from the Hebrew by Peter Cole.
p. cm.
ISBN 0-8112-1539-3
1. Shabtai, Aharon – Translations into English.
I. Cole, Peter, 1957–
II. Title.
PJ5054.S264A24 2003
892.4'16–dc21   2002155789

New Directions Books are published for James Laughlin
by New Directions Publishing Corporation
80 Eighth Avenue, New York 10011

CONTENTS

INTRODUCTION

The poems of Hebrew poet Aharon Shabtai's *J'accuse* cover a period of some six years, from the election of Benjamin Netanyahu as the prime minister of Israel in 1996 through the snipers, curfews, lynchings, sieges, suicide bombers, roadside ambushes, and extrajudicial executions of the second intifada. That uprising began on September 28, 2000, when Ariel Sharon — at the time head of the opposition Likud party — visited the Old City of Jerusalem's Muslim sanctuary known as *al-Haram al-sharif*, site of the Dome of the Rock, the al-Aqsa Mosque, and, beneath them, the ruins of the Jewish Temple. Sharon was accompanied on his tour by a large contingent of politicians and armed policemen. Violent riots broke out in the compound after Friday prayers the following day; the Israeli authorities used excessive force to quell them, and four Palestinians were killed, some two hundred injured. The mass unrest that had been predicted for several years, in the wake of the deteriorating situation in Palestinian communities and profound disappointment with the implementation of the Oslo Accords, swept across the occupied territories.

Some twenty-two months later, as I write this, the death toll in what has become known as the al-Aqsa Intifada stands at more than fourteen hundred Palestinians and nearly six hundred Israelis. Israel has declared itself to be at war, and large parts of the West Bank and Gaza have been re-occupied or are now under long-term siege. The much-vaunted "irreversible" historic process that was signed onto in the White House Rose Garden by Yitzhak Rabin, Yasser Arafat, and William Jefferson Clinton has, for all intents and purposes, been unwound.

Netanyahu's Thatcherite economics provided the unlikely subject of Shabtai's 1999 book, *Politika,* and the first third of *J'accuse* is drawn from that volume, which also mourns the final collapse of Israel's humanist, semi-socialist, pre-1967 ethos. The remainder of the poems here, beginning with two written about the now infamous shooting of twelve-year-old Muhammad al-Durra as his father tried to protect him behind a concrete barricade in Gaza, is taken from the final section of Shabtai's latest collection of Hebrew poems, *Artzenu (Our Land).* Many of the poems in that volume were first published on the weekend literary pages of Israel's daily paper of record, *Ha'aretz* – the equivalent of their being featured in the *New York Times Book Review* – and were met with angry letters to the editor and threats of canceled subscriptions. *Ha'aretz* refused to publish "J'accuse," the third poem written in the series (and perhaps the harshest and most prophetic of the lot), but "Passover 2002" was printed sometime later in a special holiday edition of the paper a few days before the biggest and most joyful celebrations of the Israeli year. There was the intellectual readership of the nation, as it prepared for large family Seders, or vacation, being told –

> You read the Haggadah
> like swine ...
> Passover, however,
> is stronger than you are.
> Go outside and see:
> the slaves are rising up ...

Lines like these have gotten Shabtai in trouble steadily throughout the thirty-five years of his publishing career, and his provocations have been unsettling, to say the least. Like Archilochus the Scold, he moves with often disturbing ease between the poles of praise and scorn, lyric flight and biological matter-of-factness. If in the Greek-Anthology-like *Domestic Poem* (1976) Shabtai takes laconic inventory of the household, celebrating its concreteness, stability, and mystery – "The kitchen contains / an Eden / of wisdom // Wisdom nests / in fire and salt / the water supply / is mythological" – a few books later, in *Love* (1986), he erupts in a dithyrambic dismantlement of that domestic-Objectivist self: the violent return of a repressed old passion leads to a transformative moment of self-recognition and, later in the poem, and throughout his next several volumes, to the most sexually explicit and ribald work in the history of modern Hebrew poetry. Here too the tutelary spirits of his poetic tack are classical, and the comic and caustic are never far apart:

> I've always missed out on the prettiest girls;
> only after they've screwed in every hole and position
> do they come to me for help with their poems, or a lesson,
> and I tell them of Phoinix, whose lips dripped pearls
>
> of wisdom and how, in exchange for the knowledge, he'd usually
> get a comfortable bed with sheets of lambskin and, if he were lucky,
> hear, in an adjacent tent – Patroklós
> making love with Iphis, and Diomêdê with Akhilleus.
>
> So I won't get to sleep with the prettiest girls.
> I'll fix their lines, put up with their stupid chatter,
> and, late at night, comfort myself as I stick my finger …
>   – from *The Heart*, 1994

The poet's primary responsibility, Shabtai makes clear, is (at least on the level of literature) freshness, attentiveness, and surprise. And when things fall apart, the responsible writer can't but apply these values to the least likely and perhaps most slippery of literary subjects – politics and public affairs. "In dark times will there also be singing?"

Bertolt Brecht asks. "Yes," he answers, "there will also be singing, about the dark times."

*

The dark times in question are clearly darkest for the Palestinian people, and Shabtai is genuinely concerned about their situation and the treatment they have long suffered. Nevertheless, the Hebrew title of his most recent volume, *Artzenu* – which can also be translated *Our Country* – reminds us that what Shabtai knows best, and what courses through his veins, is Hebrew culture. What drives him to his desk in the "dim hour / when the thud of the paper / hitting the doorstep is heard" is his understanding that the fate of the ethical Hebrew culture in which he was raised is inextricably linked to the fate of Palestinian society and the Palestinian people, which his own government is doing its best to crush. The Hebrew language, the moral underpinnings of Israeli society, the very simplicity, modesty, and dailiness that he has embraced and championed throughout his writing life in some of the most powerful and original Hebrew poetry of the past thirty years – all are now endangered: "The pure words I suckled from my mother's breasts: Man, Child, Justice, Mercy, and so on, / are dispossessed before our eyes, imprisoned in ghettos, murdered at checkpoints." To properly convey the extent of that threat and goad his reader into wakefulness, Shabtai will resort to the most theatrical of poetic gestures, and in the process risk, as he has put it, "poetic suicide."

In doing so he looks back to other poets who have found in the mechanisms of state a fitting and *necessary* subject for poetry, despite the deep-seated and often unconscious assumption of many readers that politics inevitably devours or somehow thwarts the interior life of the individual, which they deem to be the poet's proper concern. Throughout the poems of *J'accuse*, the reader will hear deliberate echoes of – or homages to – Brecht and Mandelstam, Hikmet and Akhmatova, Pound, Eluard, and numerous others. Beneath that one also notes the recovery of the moral perspective and apocalyptic tone, the universalism of the classical Hebrew prophets who raged against the corruption of the nation in biblical Samaria (Amos) and the political scene on the eve of the destruction of the First Temple (Jeremiah). Above all one feels the presence, again, of the Greek poets and dramatists whose work Shabtai has lived with and taught for some four decades now. For apart from his *enfant-terrible* poet status in Israel, Shabtai is best known for his translations of Greek tragedy and comedy, which a generation of students has studied in brilliantly annotated volumes with appendices containing large selections of Greek lyric poetry as well. *J'accuse*, one might say, involves a pan-Mediterranean application of lessons learned from all the writers listed above, as well as from the plain-spoken likes of Hesiod's eighth-century B.C. tale of the Good City and the Bad City in *Works and Days:*

> … When the judges of a town are fair
> To foreigner and citizen alike,
> Their city prospers and her people bloom;
> Since Peace is in the land, her children thrive
> …
> But there are some who till the fields of pride
> And work at evil deeds; Zeus marks them out,
>
> And often, all the city suffers for
> Their wicked schemes, and on these men, from heaven
> The son of Kronos sends great punishments …

In much of their work, as in many of the poems of *J'accuse,* the personal is not the political; instead, the political becomes the personal, and the fate of the polis is the fate of the self.

These are, then, not poems of solace in the face of the tragic, as we have come to expect in the contemporary American context. They are, rather, poems of sentence by a poet who refuses to be silent before the barbaric and the brutal. They fulfill not only the traditional functions of political poetry – witnessing, remembrance, protest – but also, in their audacity, serve as a poet's mirror held up to his people: one designed to show the nation its true reflection, now and in days to come.

PETER COLE
JERUSALEM
AUGUST 2002

J'ACCUSE

TIMES ARE BAD

Times are bad. I take an oath of loyalty to the table
coated with white Formica, a cup full of pens, the ashtray.
I dreamed that the State had passed out of existence
and with our children we'd settled down in the three volumes of the
    dictionary.
My house will stand beside the word *mix,* on the way to *morals.*
I'll risk my life for the sake of a single rectangle alone –
the bed that belongs to Tanya and me – two meters by a meter-and-a-half.
I saw the pictures of the prime minister and minister of defense
in the morning paper, smeared with a reddish lacquer, like a prostitute's
    nails.
I drive my thoughts far away from them now –
to a can of baked beans, to two sausages and Chinese parsley.

NEW LOVE

Zionism was once a pretty young thing like my cousin Tsila.
Boys caught sight of the narrow gap between her thighs – and were
  ready to die.
Ahh, what days we spent among the cypresses, not far from Wadi
  Faleek!
What proud, honest mounds of manure I lifted with Joseph Mintser at
  Kibbutz Merhavyah!
But political theses can turn into stinking corpses too,
and it's better to leave them behind – before we sink into an ethical mire –
in order to take up a new idea that might enlist the stores of goodness
  within our hearts:
namely, that equal rights be granted to the children of this land as one,
that two cultures should flourish with dignity, side by side, like beds in
  a single garden.
Let this be the girl whose legs thrill us on the eve of the year 2000,
and about whom we dream toward the summer's end, and through the
  months of winter.

THE REASON TO LIVE HERE

This country is turning into the private estate of twenty families.

Look at its fattened political arm, at the thick neck of its bloated
    bureaucracy:
these are the officers of Samaria.

There's no need to consult the oracle:
What the capitalist swine leaves behind, the nationalist hyena shreds
    with its teeth.

When the Governor of the Bank of Israel raises the interest rate by
    half-a-percent,
the rich are provided with backyard pools by the poor.

The soldier at the outpost guards the usurer, who'll put a lien on his home
when he's laid off from the privatized factory and falls behind on his
    mortgage payments.

The pure words I suckled from my mother's breasts: Man, Child,
    Justice, Mercy, and so on,
are dispossessed before our eyes, imprisoned in ghettos, murdered at
    checkpoints.

And yet, there's still good reason to stay on and live here –
to hide the surviving words in the kitchen, in the basement, or the
    bathroom.

The prophet Melampus saved twin orphaned snakes from the hand of
    his slaves:
they slithered toward his bed while he slept, then licked the auricles
    of his ears.
When he woke with a fright, he found he could follow the speech of
    birds —

so Hebrew delivered will lick the walls of our hearts.

THIS COUNTRY

This country, built by cooperatives of workers and pioneers,
this state, born beside a slice of bread and jam,
is being cut up and sold like sausage – to businessmen and venture
    capitalists.
Tomorrow, the day after tomorrow, that capital will flee,
and three days from now it will be as though it had never been.
Meanwhile, the privatizers collect their stocks, and bathe their
    behinds in champagne.
As for the privatized, some become policemen or guards,
and some are spit out of factories, laid off or on strike.
And at night, they see themselves there on the tube – the beaters and
    the beaten.

TO MY FRIEND

Apuleius, in *The Golden Ass,* writes of times like these:
A man with the head of a pig becomes king;
people mutter gibberish and turn into wolves.
Beautiful women fornicate with apes.
Rabbis shoot pistols, affix mezuzahs to a whorehouse.
Crowds drink down a rat's jokes, the hyena's howl.
New breasts are bought on the open market, one's buttocks are fixed.
The rich man farts and the nation stirs with excitement.
On the street, people wave flags made of money.
A journalist's tongue sticks out of his ass, and suddenly he's become a
    thinker.
Competitions are held between liars, ass-kissers, soldiers, and crooks.
To the sound of applause, and in front of the camera, entire villages
    are razed.
A fat man swallows a hundred thin men in public.
Thievery's adopted as the national faith, vineyards are plundered, and
    wells.
And everywhere there roams the officer, jailer, tax collector, informer.
Ships full of slaves anchor at port.
The hangman sits at the head of the table, surrounded by an entourage
    of professors.
A secret policeman is the day's astrologer, the Bank's Governor
    becomes our alchemist.
But all these delusions disappear in an instant; a few days of rain is
    enough,
and the idols of authority, the monsters of weaponry, the masks – all
    are down in the mud.

Men remove their ape suits and wolf skins, and get back to work.

And we, too, my friend: for your grandfather and mine didn't live on blood.

For a thousand years, and a thousand more, we broke our bread with the poor of the earth.

Come – let's saddle our donkeys, let's go back and bake this bread:

you – for the honest men of Izmir, and I – for the diligent Alexandrians.

THE MORAL, IT SEEMS, DOESN'T COME WITH A SMILE

The moral, it seems, doesn't come with a smile, like an uncle with pieces
    of candy.
Only when fire flares up in the wheat are the fattened serpents burned.
As for the wheat itself, the fine, innocent wheat – what a shame!
Only when the wealthy are drowning in the tears of the poor will it
    come.
These tears are slowly gathering, and only gradually becoming a sea;
meanwhile, they're used to water a pumpkin, give drink to a beast in the
    alley;
we shower with them and wash our clothes, office floors are mopped
    with them.
So build more towers, more steel doors and walls of glass –
let the waters rise and drown the man shaving up in the penthouse.
For only when the stick strikes the hump will the heart begin to listen.

SUMMER 1997

Summer has come, the long season. Indifferently
the grass on the hill withers, goodness dwindles.
Look at the shoemaker, there in the doorway:
the scrawl across his brow is saying
that the wells of morality have all gone dry, the wine of mercy run out.
Now sweaty rubber soles will rejoice, and the flies,
yes, the flies for which words are no reproach,
swarm by swarm will come and sit on the wounds of my hairless pate.
Thank God that I, an aging poet, fifty-eight,
can bend my back and turn myself into a horse.

LOTEM ABDEL SHAFI

The heart dies without space for love, without a moral horizon:
think of it then as a bird trapped in a box.
My heart goes out with love to those beyond the fence;
only toward them can one really advance, that is, make progress.
Without them I feel I'm half a person.
Romeo was born a Montague, and Juliet came from the Capulet line,
and I'm a disciple of Shakespeare, not Ben Gurion –
therefore I'll be delighted if my daughter marries the grandson of
    Haidar Abdel Shafi.
I mean this, of course, as a parable only – but the parable is my measure,
and since it has more to do with my body than teeth or hair,
this isn't just some idle fancy that, out of poetic license,
I place our fate in my daughter's sex.
That I grant myself this imaginary gift, testifies to the extent
to which we're living, still, in the underworld,
where we're granted the hope and potential of an amoeba.
But all mythology begins with creatures that creep and crawl,
spring out of the ground and devour each other,
until a sacred union occurs, healing the breach in the world.
The Arab groom from Gaza, too, will extend to my daughter a dress
on which is embroidered the Land redeemed from Apartheid's curse –
our Land as a whole, belonging equally to all of its offspring,
and then he'll lift the veil from her face, and say to her:
"And now I take you to be my wife, Lotem Abdel Shafi."

POLITICS

Your arms which I kiss where they meet the breast,
your white legs which branch like vines, with the sex's amulet,
the open plain of your belly, your eyes, lips, and neck –
they are benevolence, brotherhood, the quivering revelation of truth;
they are justice, equality, the freedom to want and think;
they're the bestowal of opportunity, the work which is love.
With the raising of the knees they put tyranny, coarseness, and hatred
    to shame;
they are uprightness and candor, the pride that puts nothing down;
they're the communal revealed in the personal – the desire to share;
they're the revolt against all idiocy, against all ignorance and sanctimony;
they're the pleasure of giving, of getting, of having enough;
they're the beauty that cannot be purchased with money, but only with joy;
they are what counters oppression, occupation, exploitation – they are
    morality's bliss;
they are affinity, faith, the devotion that holds no fear;
the availability of basic needs, of education, the recognition of mutual
    dignity;
they are the right to strike, do nothing, demonstrate, oppose.
All that is good and worthy of humanity is here for me to see and touch,
and this, this is my politics – tender-limbed – lying in bed before me.

CULTURE

The mark of Cain won't sprout
from a soldier who shoots
at the head of a child
on a knoll by the fence
around a refugee camp —
for beneath his helmet,
conceptually speaking,
his head is made of cardboard.
On the other hand,
the officer has read *The Rebel;*
his head is enlightened,
and so he does not believe
in the mark of Cain.
He's spent time in museums,
and when he aims
his rifle at a boy
as an ambassador of Culture,
he updates and recycles
Goya's etchings
and *Guernica.*

ROSH HASHANAH

Even after the murder
of the child Muhammad on Rosh HaShanah,
the paper didn't go black.
In the same water in which the snipers
wash their uniforms,
I prepare my pasta,
and over it pour
olive oil in which I've browned
pine nuts,
which I cooked for two minutes with dried tomatoes,
crushed garlic, and a tablespoon of basil.
As I eat, the learned minister of foreign affairs
and public security
appears on the screen,
and when he's done
I write this poem.
For that's how it's always been –
the murderers murder,
the intellectuals make it palatable,
and the poet sings.

NOSTALGIA

The dumpy little man
with the scourge in his hand,
in his free time
runs his fingers
over the keys of a baby grand –
but we've seen it all before.
And so, from the primitive East
we return to the West.
He'll help solve the economy's problems:
the unemployed will man the tanks,
or dig graves,
and, come evening,
we'll listen to Schubert and Mozart.
O my country, my country,
with each sandal,
with each thread
of my khaki pants,
I've loved you –
I could compose
psalms to a salad
of white cheese and scallions.
But now, who will I meet
when I go out for dinner?

Gramsci's jailers?
What clamor will rise
up through the window facing the street?
And when it's all over,
my dear, dear reader,
on which benches will we have to sit,
those of us who shouted "Death to the Arabs!"
and those who claimed they "didn't know"?

J'ACCUSE

The sniper who shot at Muhammad the child
beneath his father's arm
wasn't acting alone –
someone else in uniform,
a junior cog in the wheel who was briefed
at a higher level,
positioned him there on the roof,
a public servant,
a cantor
for the Days of Awe;
and someone else
manufactured the ammunition,
and another had it distributed
like bars of chocolate.
The tree doesn't go green
when a single leaf unfurls,
many wrinkled brows
leaned over the plans.
History has known
foreheads like these –
technicians of slaughter,
bastards in whose eyes
morality is a pain in the ass.
But even cucumbers
need dirt and a little dung.
The worm isn't born of air;
a million words are required

to reconstruct the manner
in which public discourse itself
is corrupted and turned into refuse –
that which within the body politic
was created to preserve
the heart of justice.

But now
there isn't time for any of that,
when right in front of the cameras,
without any shame,
grown men in uniforms
are shooting into a helpless crowd.
From the back with their necks and behinds
they look like guys at the airgun range
by the screen at an amusement park,
trying to win their girlfriends
a doll or a box of candy.
Atop a hill,
at the distance dictated
by the administrators' handbook,
the prime minister looks on
with his company of advisers.
They gaze down
into the Vale of Tears,
toward the horde which is scrambling
like jackals and rabbits,
grandchildren
and great-grandchildren of refugees

who were stripped of their homes and fields,
wells and towns,
and with an iron hand were driven
into enclaves and ghettos.
Each one of these authorities
sees to his part in the plan:
one's in charge of liquidation,
another of the daily harassment;
this one's field is public relations,
that one's collaboration;
this one deals with expulsion and fencing,
that one with the destruction of homes.
Because, when it comes down to it, we're only speaking
of a population of a certain size,
which needs to be pounded and ground
then shipped off as human powder.
The outrage itself has to be packaged
like any piece of merchandise,
with all the clichés
of corporate politics:
they'll give it a name,
then a format can be arranged
for staged negotiations,
with "breakthroughs" and "concessions,"
and moments of press-covered heightened tension,
complete with a pr blitz full of talk:
for this purpose we have the spokesman,
the journalist and author as well,
the TV announcer and the professor,

a long lineup of Men of Letters,
all blowing into the Process's trumpets — .
For the sniper who fired at the child
is only a single stinking instrument
within an enormous orchestra,
which is conducted by the man who knows
more than anyone else
that long-term solutions can be found
for any and every problem,
when it's no longer breathing.
The moment that man smiles,
the skin over skulls becomes transparent;
when, hoarsely, he pronounces
the word "Peace" —
mothers wake up trembling;
he knows that words
are only the skins of potatoes
with which the stupid are to be stuffed —
and now, at long last,
he'll roll up his sleeves
and get down to the work at which he excels,
and bring about a blood bath.

WAR

I, too, have declared war:
You'll need to divert part of the force
deployed to wipe out the Arabs –
to drive them out of their homes
and expropriate their land –
and set it against me.
You've got tanks and planes,
and soldiers by the battalion;
you've got the rams' horns in your hands
with which to rouse the masses;
you've got men to interrogate and torture;
you've got cells for detention.
I have only this heart
with which I give shelter
to an Arab child.
Aim your weapons at it:
even if you blow it apart
it will always,
always mock you.

AS WE WERE MARCHING

Two days ago in Rafi'ah,
nine Arabs were killed,
yesterday six
were killed in Hebron,
and today — just two.
Last year
as we were marching
from Shenkin Street,
a man on a motorcycle
shouted toward us:
"Death to the Arabs!"
At the corner of Labor,
opposite the Bezalel Market,
next to Braun's
butcher shop,
and at the corner of Bograshov:
"Death to the Arabs!"
For a full year
this poem was lying
on the sidewalk
along King George Street,
and today
I lift it up and compose
its final line:
"*Life* to the Arabs!"

PEACE

What nerve
these empty people have!
They've taken the word
peace by the hair
dragged it out
of its humble bed,
and turned it into their whore
beside the Central Bus Station.
After they had their way,
they turned the State
into a couch
upon which she screws around the clock.
In the morning she sucks off a sniper in uniform,
and at evening he returns
and proudly displays
the X he etched
into the butt of his rifle,
after he'd shot dead
a young woman, age 19,
who was hanging up laundry
on her roof in Hebron.

ELECTIONS: ISRAEL 2001

I'm for Peepee,
long live Peepee!
Peepee's mission is civilized,
cultured, salubrious.
Peepee makes sure
that the blood flows smoothly –
clean, and for a good reason.
Therefore, thanks to Peepee,
words give off a pleasant scent.
Not for nothing do the
leading writers and professors
express their support for Peepee.

I'm for Caca.
Caca resembles
earth that swallows
the choice words
stuck to the brow
of every
terminated target.
Caca does
what Peepee does,
but – with greater boldness,
without hiding

behind professors.
The truth in fact stinks,
but it's beautiful in its solid state.
Therefore, I'm for Caca.
Long live Caca!

THE FIFTEENTH OF JANUARY

On the thirty-first of December,
the dentist and activist
for peace,
Dr. Thabet Thabet,
was gunned down
and now it's January fifteenth,
and years ago on this date
soldiers tossed
Rosa Luxemburg's corpse
into a Berlin canal.
From the dawn of that mad war she called
"Don't shoot!"
and therefore was expelled
from the Socialist Party
and locked up in
five prisons.
She knew
every plant by name
and identified each
bird by its twitter.
A pigeon with a wounded wing
she took up
from the window of her cell
at the Breslau jail,
and after it healed
the bird would wait
each day

for her walk in the prison yard,
then circle round
the small woman
or stand beside her
when she sat down to rest
on the gravel.
When she was ill,
he'd fly toward her bed
behind the bars,
and soon after
an entourage of birds would follow.
Her visitors carried
food she'd saved
(and denied herself)
for Leo Jogiches,
her lover held
in Moabit Prison.
She said: "The main thing is
to be good —
that resolves
and ties up everything,
and is better than all
cleverness and knowing."
History's repeated
with its saints and war-mongers
joined in a drama
on the ceiling of the sky
which darkens now
over our heads —

and I wonder,
Chief of Staff Mofaz,
and General Bugi Ya'alon,
if you'd have sent
a chopper
to blow up her room
(with a missile)
at the offices of *The Red Flag*,
or, with more perfect
surgical precision,
have parked a truck
outside her suburban apartment
and when she left it
to go to her car
taken her out with snipers' bullets
from a range of two hundred meters
as in Tul Karem?

THE NEW JEW

The new Jew,
der neue Jude,
rises at night,
puts his uniform on,
kisses his wife and child,
and, in two or three hours, destroys
a quarter in one of Gaza's ghettos.
He manages to make it back
in time for coffee and rolls.
In the paper,
the fresh picture of women and children
picking through islands of rubble,
like frightened hens,
pales beside
the shuttle within
that professional gesture.

All the while, above, a helicopter
observes the grounded humanity
of those who laugh
when they are tickled,
and bleed when they
are shot by snipers,
and, in memory's skies –
packed with clichés
and plays on words –
it outlines a lazy spiral,

enclosing once and for all
identity within parentheses.
Whether it be with a barbed-wire fence
or with a ring of outposts:
identity becomes the ghetto,
and the ghetto becomes identity.

TO A PILOT

When next you circle
in your chopper
over Jenin,
pilot, remember the children
and old women
in the homes at which you fire.
Spread a layer
of chocolate across your missile,
and do your best to be precise –
so their souvenir will be sweet
when the walls start to fall.

THE TREES ARE WEEPING

for Tu biShevat

The trees are weeping
in the Land of Israel.
Rome's soldiers are razing
acre after acre;
there is no compassion
for the land's raiment —
its seven species.
The trees will all
be sold to a broker;
they won't be made
into crosses
for Jesus and Barabbas.
And on these parcels of land
concessions will be granted
to Burger King   -
and Kentucky Fried Chicken.

A POEM ABOUT NETA GOLAN

In 1938,
after he was put
onto a destroyer
and sentenced
to twenty-eight years in jail
on the charge of inciting
Turkish sailors
to rebellion,
the poet Nazim Hikmet
was thrown
into the back
of the ship's latrine.
Before the eyes of his torturers,
he stood
knee-deep in excrement
and, nearly fainting,
and about to keel
over on account of the stench,
he opened his mouth
and began to sing
songs of romance,
the ballads of farmers,
and every melody he could remember.
And so, as Neruda tells it,
his powers returned
to him with pride.

My dear Nazim,
I'll learn from you
and sing today
of Neta Golan —
who was thrown
into Kishon Prison
for binding herself
to an olive tree
before the army's bulldozers
at the village of Istiyya.
Thanks to Neta
I won't collapse today
into the sewage of Ariel Sharon.

THE VICTORY OF BEIT JALLA

*"Realistic people for whom despair
feeds the devouring fire of hope"*
— Eluard

A slap of the hand
will disperse the soldiers
like a swarm of flies.

The hills will bare
their well-scrubbed rears,
and the sun will polish the rooftops.

Eight-year-olds, ten-year-olds,
children aged eleven,
will emerge from their monastery lock-up.

Behind corners and under the beds,
they'll drop their stones
and, out in the alley,

one will gather his eye,
another the stump of his hand.

Into the back yard
our scarecrows' junk will be thrown.

In the village of Beit Jalla,
we'll fall in all humility
onto the blackened necks
of our parents' parents –

here's the peasant
with the graying stubble
riding on the back of a donkey

wearing the glasses
with the cracked lens
of Joseph Posner!

We too will be refugees.
We'll sit shyly
at the edge of a blanket
spread out beneath an olive tree,
and, together,
eat hummus and a cucumber.

TO DR. MAJED NASSAR

The e-mail hasn't stopped for a minute. For three
days now, like a foul wave, a pogrom
has been sweeping over six towns. Donations
of blood were gathered by a doctor from Beit Sahour

for Bethlehem's wounded, but they can't get through.
Tanks have surrounded the hospital, and so, instead,
straight from Manger Square, they've brought him a dead
boy killed by an army sniper. Dear Dr. Nassar,

could words send a shiver through a sniper's finger?
Will tears buy a bandage? You stopped counting
(you wrote today) your injured, some of whom are

lying out there still …
Is it any comfort to know that the tanks murdering
in my name are digging a grave for my people as well?

RAADA

Yesterday, at the edge of the village of Sanour, a pack
of army snipers killed Raada. She was picking
olives in the grove with her family, early in the morning.
She died on the spot, a bullet lodged in her neck.

Eighteen years old. "A child with a heart of gold,"
her mother said. "At home, in the groves, she was always
helping out. Her whole life was ahead of her,
and they killed her, just like that – in cold blood."

I think of Raada – and the sugar cane that my brother
used to carve into honey-like tidbits,
and the bread sliced, along with a radish, by my mother

who would set it out for me and him,
as I remember them, turn in my throat to vomit –
not just the uniform, the flag, and the national anthem.

BASEL SQUARE

After months abroad,
I strolled down to Basel Square
and the store run
by the grocer from Wadi Ara.
That same smile
on a devastated face
flickered at the edge
of a shopkeeper's mouth,
or a barber's,
along Alexanderplatz
during the thirties.
With a feeble grip like this
they shook the hands
of clients,
members of the master race,
who deigned to drop in.
And this is what drives
the sleep from my eyes
and forces me
to rise and go back to the table
in this dim hour
when the thud of the paper
hitting the doorstep is heard.

TOY SOLDIERS

And why didn't you bring flowers,
a truck loaded down with bouquets
for the impoverished children of Rafi'ah?
Or sacks of cheap sweaters for the mothers
or Chinese lighters for the fathers?
And why didn't you waken them
with a bundle of umbrellas and raincoats?
Or a jeep full of fireworks to spread, for a moment,
a canopy of splendor over the puddles?
Haven't you read Andersen's "The Flying Trunk"?
You could have used the bulldozer's maw
to shovel bread to the doors of the houses.
To deposit cartons of milk in secret.
Don't you know how to surprise?
Don't your brains contain even an ounce of imagination?
You could easily have used the cover
of darkness to build a playground in silence,
or put back the electric poles in the alleys
or stock the clinic with drugs!
Haven't you heard of Louis Pasteur?
What muck have you filled your heads with,
that you came by night in the driving rain
to tear down seventy miserable shanties
and toss seven hundred people –
women and children – into the mud?
Idiotic soldiers of lead,
was your father a knife

that only knows how to chop?
Or your mother a pair of scissors
that only knows how to sever?

MY HEART

My lips mutter: Palestine! Do not die on me!
My heart's with each syringe in your hand, Moustafa Barghouti!

It's with the Muqata'a, with the roadside corpse that help couldn't
    reach –
with the pencil on your table, Mahmoud Darwish.

With the empty oxygen tanks at the clinic in Nablus.
Maha Abu Shareef, the soldiers who stormed into your house

pissed on the walls of my heart as well.
And now, for the wheels of a Red Crescent ambulance, that heart has
    become a footstool,

and for you too, Manaal Sufyaan, at Ayn Masbach,
lying in a pool of blood, shot by thugs on your porch.

Our country, a new birth is underway in Bethlehem –
the bloody placenta will be tossed into a pail, and from the womb

a creature born of our people's love will burst forth into the blue.
Listen, his heart is beating through mine – I'm a Palestinian Jew.

OUR LAND

I remember how,
in 1946, hand in hand
we went out into the field
at the edge of Frishman Street
to learn about Autumn.
Under the rays of the sun
slanting through the October clouds
a *fallah* was cutting a furrow
with a wooden plough.
His friend wore a *jallabiya*
rolled up to his knees
as he crouched on a knoll.
Soon we will all
meet in the Tel Aviv below –
Weinstein the milkman,
and Haim the iceman,
Solganik
and the staff at the dry-goods co-op:
Hannah and Frieda and Tzitron;
and the one-armed man
from the clothing store
at the corner
near Café Ditza;
Dr. Levova
and Nurse Krasnova;
the gentle
Dr. Gottlieb.

And we'll meet Stoller
the butcher,
and his son Baruch;
and Muzikant the barber,
and Lauterbach, the librarian;
and the pretty dark-skinned lady
from the Hahn Restaurant.
And we'll meet the street-sweeper
Mr. Yaretzky,
whose widow had hanging
in her hallway
the parable-painting
showing the stages of life.
For these *fallahin* as well,
and also for the children of the village of Sumel,
who herded goats
on Frug Street,
the heart will make room
like a table
opening its wings.
For we belong
to a single body –
Arabs and Jews.
Tel Aviv and Tulkarem,
Haifa and Ramallah –
what *are* they
if not a single pair of shoulders,
twin breasts?
We quarreled

like the body parts of the man
who brought the milk of the lioness
down from the mountains
in the legend told by Bialik.
Through the cracks in the earth,
we'll look up at you then;
under your feet
our land is being harrowed
with chains of steel,
and above your heads there is no sky
like a light-blue shirt –
but only the broad buttocks of the murderer.

PASSOVER 2002

Instead of scalding
your pots and plates,
take steel wool
to your hearts:
You read the Haggadah
like swine, which
if put before a table
would forage about in the bowl
for parsley and dumplings.
Passover, however,
is stronger than you are.
Go outside and see:
the slaves are rising up,
a brave soul
is burying its oppressor
beneath the sand.
Here is your cruel,
stupid Pharaoh,
dispatching his troops
with their chariots of war,
and here is the Sea of Freedom,
which swallows them.

I LOVE PASSOVER

I love Passover,
since that's when you'll be back.
Like every year,
we'll take the car to Kiryat Motzkin
and, over glasses of wine
and bowls of *charoset*,
Zvi will tell us
of the March of Death.
Then we'll return to Tel Aviv,
and as you drive in the dark,
the car's windows
will fog up,
and I'll put my hand on your knee.
At home, we'll get into bed
and celebrate our own
private Seder.
I see myself putting
my lips to your belly
and thinking of honey,
while in the street below
our angel passes.

NOTES

These notes have been prepared to aid readers not familiar with the particulars of the situation described in the poems. Sources have been cited for information related to the events on the ground, in large part because so much of what Shabtai says will be hard for many Americans to hear and may strike them as simply "inaccurate."

The al-Aqsa Intifada information is taken from the Mitchell Report (www.mideastweb.org/mitchell_report.htm) and B'tselem: The Israeli Information Center for Human Rights in the Occupied Territories (www.btselem.org/English/Statistics/Al_Aqsa_Fatalities.asp). For more on the shooting of Muhammed al-Durra, see Anat Cygielman, *Ha'aretz*, November 7, 2000.

Archilochus: see Guy Davenport's *7 Greeks*, New Directions, 1995.

Quotations of Shabtai's previous poetry: from *Love & Selected Poems*, translated by Peter Cole, Sheep Meadow Press, 1997.

Amos: see, for example, 4:1–2: "Hear this word, you cows of Bashan [see Ps. 22:12], who are in the mountain of Samaria, who oppress the poor, who crush the needy …"; or Amos 6:1–7: "Woe to those who are at ease in Zion, and to those who feel secure on the mountain of Samaria.… O you who put far away the evil day, and bring near the seat of violence …"

Jeremiah: see, for example, 7:2–15, the Temple sermon: "Amend your ways and your doings, and I will cause you to dwell in this place. Trust ye not in lying words, saying: 'The Temple of the Lord, the temple of the Lord, the temple of the Lord are these.' Nay, but if ye thoroughly amend your ways and your doings; if ye thoroughly execute justice between a man and his neighbor; if ye oppress not the stranger, the fatherless, and the widow, and shed not innocent blood in this place … then will I cause you to dwell in this place, in the land that I gave to your fathers, for ever and ever."

Hesiod and Theognis, translated by Dorothea Wender, Penguin, 1973. There are also numerous parallels in the poems of Solon and Theognis written in the elegiac meter (Solon: "I know, and my heart within me is crushed with sorrow, / that before my eyes the mother of all the Ionians, my country / is being destroyed ..."). Shabtai has stated that he sees the Hebrew poems of *J'accuse* as elegies that embody a *nostos* for a vanished Israeliness and diasporic Judaism's talent for tolerance.

"New Love"

Wadi Faleek: A Palestinian area close to the village where the poet's family lived. Today in the vicinity of the city of Herzliya.

Joseph Mintser: A Kibbutz Merhavyah member from an educated, well-to-do Galician family.

Kibbutz Merhavyah: A kibbutz in the Jezreel Valley in northern Israel. Founded in 1929 by Polish pioneers from the HaShomer HaTza'ir movement, which was, and still is, a Zionist-socialist youth movement. "HaShomer HaTza'ir sought to create a synthesis between Jewish culture and the rebuilding and defending of Eretz Israel on the one hand, and universal cultural and philosophical values, on the other" (*Encyclopedia Judaica*). The poet went to high school in Merhavyah, and his second collection of poems, *Kibbutz*, treats the details of life there.

"The Reason to Live Here"

Samaria: Capital of the northern kingdom of Israel in the ninth and eighth centuries B.C.E., following the split of the Israelite kingdom after the death of Solomon. Now the Hebrew name for the northern part of the West Bank, in the biblicizing terminology of the Greater Israel movement and the Israeli government.

Melampus: In Greek mythology, the first mortal endowed with prophetic powers (Bullfinch). The story of the serpents is told in Apollodorus I:9.11.

"This Country"

Privatization: Israel was founded as a highly centralized state, with most national infrastructure sectors being administered by government-owned companies and trade unions. Health care, food staples, public transportation, and higher education were heavily subsidized. Dismantlement of that system began in the eighties, and continues still. It has played a major role in redefining the nature of Israeli society. For more information see the Israeli government Ministry of Finance web site: www.mof.gov.il / mof3.htm.

"Lotem Abdel Shafi"

All marriages in Israel are administered by the orthodox religious authorities; civil marriages performed in Israel, let alone marriages across religious lines, are not recognized by law.

Ben Gurion: David Ben Gurion headed the struggle for Jewish independence in Palestine and was the first prime minister and minister of defense of the State of Israel. He served as prime minister for thirteen years in all, and his name is now synonymous with the founding of the state.

Haidar Abdel Shafi: b. 1919, Gaza. A prominent Palestinian politician, he was spokesman of the first Palestinian Legislative Council in 1962–63 and headed the Palestinian delegation to the Madrid Conference. His eloquent opening statement there is a good introduction to the man. Elected to the Palestinian Legislative Council in 1996 with the greatest number of votes of any candidate, he resigned in September 1997 to protest what he perceived to be the undemocratic and inefficient policies of the Palestinian Authority.

The dress: These lines allude to Pherecydes' description of the wedding of Zas and Cthonie, when, as an allegory of the act of creation, Zas embroidered a great cloth depicting Ge (Earth) and Ogenos (Okeanos). See *The Presocratic Philosophers,* Kirk, Raven and Schofield (Cambridge), pp. 60–62.

"Culture"

Sniper: Information on snipers in the IDF is taken, in large part, from the Israeli daily press, which has run numerous news and feature stories on the sharpshooter units, especially the casualties they inflict on children. See, for example, the articles by Amira Hass in *Ha'aretz:* "Don't Shoot Till You Can See They're Over the Age of 12," on January 30, 2002, and prior to that on July 26, 2001. See also, Chris Hedges in *Harper's,* October 2001, Arieh O'Sullivan in *The Jerusalem Post,* October 27, 2000, and Suzanne Goldenberg in *The Guardian,* May 12, 2001.

"Rosh HaShanah"

Muhammad: See introduction, page viii.

The learned minister: Shlomo Ben Ami, a professor of history and one-time ambassador to Spain, whom Prime Minister Barak made minister of public security and later minister of foreign affairs.

"Nostalgia"

The dumpy little man: A description of Ehud Barak, who is known for his high IQ, his piano playing, and his hobby of taking watches apart and reassembling them.

"War"

The addressee is Ehud Barak.

"As We Were Marching"

Rafi'ah: A neighborhood in Gaza.

Shenkin: Shenkin, Labor, Bograshov, and King George are all streets in Tel Aviv.

Death to the Arabs: A slogan often chanted at soccer games and after terrorist bombings, and commonly encountered as graffiti.

"Elections 2001"

The two candidates in this election were Ehud Barak and Ariel Sharon. There was a widespread movement among the left to cast blank ballots in protest at the lack of a better alternative. Shabtai's poem appeared in *Ha'aretz* just prior to election day.

"The Fifteenth of January"

Dr. Thabet: Thabet was Fatah's general secretary in Tul Karem, director general of the Palestinian Ministry of Health, and a lecturer in Public Health at Al-Quds University. Among the early supporters of the peace process launched in Madrid in 1991, he was, as Hanan Ashwari has written, "effective in legitimizing the pursuit of peace among his constituency as well as among the Palestinian public at large." He was killed on December 31, 2000 by Israeli sniper fire outside his home in the West Bank town of Tul Karem. The father of three, he was 48. The IDF took responsibility for the killing. An Israeli military spokesman said that Israeli soldiers were responding to shooting in the area and Dr. Thabet was an unfortunate casualty of these clashes. In affidavits collected from witnesses and neighbors by al-Haq – the Ramallah-based human rights organization – there is no evidence of there having been any other disturbances in the area at the time. (See: www.alhaq.org/releases/pr_001231.html.) Writing on the following day in *Ha'aretz*, Amira Hass noted that "the killing carried many of the hallmarks of recent Israeli hit operations against senior Palestinian military operatives. Prime Minister Ehud Barak, too, hinted that Thabet's death may have been another "hit operation." See Tanya Reinhart, *Israel/Palestine: How to End the War of 1948* (Seven Stories Press, 2002), pp. 124–25.

"To a Pilot"

Jenin: Palestinian city in the northern West Bank and home to a large refugee camp founded in 1953. Large parts of it were destroyed in an IDF attack in May 2002. See the *Time* article by Matt Rees, May 13, 2002, and the report by Human Rights Watch: www.hrw.org/press/ 2002/05/jenino503.htm. Also: the interview with Moshe Nissim, one of the IDF armored bulldozer drivers in Jenin, in an article by Tsadok Yeheskeli, *Yediot Aharanot*, May 31, 2002. *Yediot* is the Israeli daily with the largest circulation. (English translation available at www.gush-shalom.org/archives/kurdi_eng.html.)

"The Trees Are Weeping"

Tu biShevat: A Jewish holiday, also known as the New Year of Trees. Literally, the fifteenth of Shevat, the fifth month in the Hebrew calendar. The festival evolved in part from a kabbalistic rite that in turn derived from an esoteric interpretation of the biblical verse, "For man is like the tree of the field" (Deuteronomy 20:19). It is now celebrated as Arbor Day and marked by the ceremonial planting of trees.

Seven species: Seven foods characteristic of the Land of Israel in Deuteronomy 8:8: "For the Lord thy God bringeth thee into a good land ... a land of wheat and barley, and vines and fig-trees and pomegranates; a land of olive-trees and honey," with honey there indicating dates.

"A Poem About Neta Golan"

Neta Golan: One of Israel's most prominent peace activists. She has been beaten by the police, had her arm broken, and was among the forty international peace observers holed up in Yasser Arafat's office in Ramallah during the siege of May 2002.

"Victory of Beit Jalla"

Beit Jalla: A West Bank town between Jerusalem and Bethlehem, held under long-term siege by the IDF. For details of the situation and its background, see:
• *www.seruv.org.il/testimonies/al_aida_eng.htm*
• *www.mfa.gov.il/mfa/go.asp?MFAH0Keu0*
and Yigal Bronner, "A Journey to Beit Jalla," *Counterpunch*, May 3, 2002.

Joseph Posner: The poet's undistinguished great uncle, in this case a representative figure of the simple Jewish immigrant-worker.

"To Dr. Majed Nassar"

Dr. Nassar: A prominent Palestinian physician and public health official from Beit Sahour. Co-author of *Cry Freedom: The Palestinian Intifada*, Bailasan Design, Ramallah, 2002. (Also sometimes spelled Majid Nasser.)

Beit Sahour: An Arab village near Bethlehem.

"Basel Square"

Basel Square: A square in north Tel Aviv.

Wadi Ara: An Arab area in northern Israel. The Palestinian grocer in question would make the trip to Tel Aviv daily with his family.

Alexanderplatz: Berlin's most famous square, later destroyed in the war. In Victor Klemperer's diaries, which the poet read while writing many of these poems, Klemperer describes the reactions of Jewish shopkeepers to the events of the late thirties in Berlin.

"My Heart"

Dr. Moustafa Barghouti: Prominent Palestinian physician and human-rights activist, president of the Union of Palestinian Medical Relief Committees, and a long-time member of Physicians for Human Rights. After addressing an international delegation on the impact of the Israeli blockade on health care in the occupied territories, he was arrested for illegal presence in the city (where he was born), beaten by Israeli security personnel, who broke his kneecap, then released at a Jerusalem police station with no charges having been brought against him. Not to be confused with Marwan Barghouti, leader of the Palestinian Tanzim.

Mahmoud Darwish: The leading Palestinian poet and a major figure in the world of contemporary Arabic letters.

Muqata'a: The Arabic name for the Ramallah compound that houses the Palestinian Authority's offices, including those of Yasser Arafat.

Ayn Masbach: A neighborhood in Nablus.

"Our Land"

fallah: Arabic for peasant or farmer, plural *fallahin.*

jallabiya: Arabic for the cotton gown or robe worn by men.

Bialik's legend: A children's story by the poet Haim Nahman Bialik that illustrates the Solomonic verse from Proverbs 18:21: "Death and life are in the power of the tongue." In the story, the King of Moab is ordered by his doctor to obtain the milk of a live lioness in order to cure a malady that was devouring him. When his own men say that the task is beyond them, he turns to Solomon, king of the neighboring lands. One of Solomon's men cleverly works out a plan, obtains the milk from the lioness, then delivers it to the messengers from Moab. The messengers head for home, the cure in hand. That night, in a dream, the leader of the group hears the parts of the body arguing over which is supreme – the legs, the hand, the eyes, the heart, the tongue, and so on. He wakes up and makes his way back with his men to Moab. When he finally presents the milk to the King, he finds himself saying, despite himself: "My Lord, we have just now returned and brought, as you requested, the milk of the bitch-dog." The King recoils in anger and sentences him to die. On the way to the gallows, as all the parts of the body are trembling in fear, the tongue says to them: "And now do you see who rules supreme?"

"Passover 2002"

Traditional Jewish families either use separate kitchen utensils for the Passover holiday or make their ordinary utensils kosher, usually by immersing them in boiling water.

"I Love Passover"

Kiryat Motzkin: A suburb in northern Israel, along the coast, where a cousin of the poet's wife lives and holds a small Seder each year. The cousin is a survivor of the camps.

Charoset: Fruit and nut paste, mixed with spices and wine. Part of the Seder rite, it symbolizes the mortar used by the slaves in Egypt.

March of Death: In January 1945, with the Soviet Army headed toward Cracow and Auschwitz, the Nazis sent 58,000 concentration camp inmates on a forced march through the snow toward camps in Germany. Most of the marchers were murdered or died en route.

BIOGRAPHICAL NOTES

AHARON SHABTAI, born 1939, is one of Israel's leading poets. He studied Greek and Philosophy at the Hebrew University, the Sorbonne, and Cambridge, and from 1972 to 1985 taught Theater Studies in Jerusalem. He currently teaches at Tel Aviv University. The foremost Hebrew translator of Greek drama, Shabtai was awarded the Prime Minister's Prize for Translation in 1993. He is the author of more than fifteen books of poetry, most recently *Our Land: Collected Poems 1987–2002*. English translations of his work have appeared in numerous journals, including *The American Poetry Review, The London Review of Books, Parnassus in Review,* and others. A large selection of his poems, *Love & Selected Poems,* was published in 1997 by Sheep Meadow Press.

PETER COLE has published two collections of poetry, *Rift* and *Hymns & Qualms*, and many volumes of translations from contemporary and medieval Hebrew and Arabic. He has received numerous awards for his work, including fellowships from the National Endowment for the Arts, the National Endowment for the Humanities, and – for his *Selected Poems of Shmuel HaNagid* – the 1998 Modern Language Association Translation Award. *Selected Poems of Solomon Ibn Gabirol* received the 2001 *T.L.S.* Hebrew Translation Prize. A 2003 Guggenheim Fellow, he lives in Jerusalem, where he edits Ibis Editions.